Taxonomies

Taxonomies

Demi-sonnets by Erin Murphy

Word Poetry

© 2022 by Erin Murphy

Published by Word Poetry
P.O. Box 541106
Cincinnati, OH 45254-1106

ISBN: 9781625494047

Poetry Editor: Kevin Walzer
Business Editor: Lori Jareo

Visit us on the web at www.wordpoetrybooks.com

Acknowledgments

Thank you to the editors of the following journals who originally published these demi-sonnets, sometimes with different titles and formatting:

"Taxonomy of Fairy Tales," "Taxonomy of Recipes," "Taxonomy of Tears," "Taxonomy of Shadows," "Taxonomy of Spills," "Taxonomy of Endings That Are Actually Beginnings," *The Laurel Review*

"Taxonomy of Mouths," "Taxonomy of Ears," "Taxonomy of Silence," "Taxonomy of Gloves," Taxonomy of Late Arrivals," "Taxonomy of Things That Slide," "Taxonomy of Smiles," *Contrary*

"Taxonomy of Overheard Conversations," "Taxonomy of Physical Markings," "Taxonomy of In-Between," *Quartet*

"Taxonomy of Needles," "Taxonomy of Churning," "Taxonomy of Full Disclosures," *MacQueen's Quinterly*

"Taxonomy of Pre-Existing Conditions," "Taxonomy of Quests," "Taxonomy of Shields," *The Citron Review*

"Taxonomy of Google Autocomplete: *What's the Difference—*," "Taxonomy of Google Autocomplete: *How Long—*," "Taxonomy of Google Autocomplete: *How Far—*," "Taxonomy of Google Autocomplete: *How Many—*," *Sledgehammer*

"Taxonomy of Knots," *DASH Literary Journal*

"Taxonomy of the Border I," "Taxonomy of the Border II," *Résonance*

"Taxonomy of Canals," "Taxonomy of Mica," "Taxonomy of Moths," "Taxonomy of Rivers," *Alba*

"Taxonomy of Rasps," *Artemis*

"Taxonomy of Places My Work Has Appeared or is Forthcoming," "Taxonomy of Turbulence," "Taxonomy of Wounds," *Shot Glass Journal*

"Taxonomy of Dancing," "Taxonomy of Emptiness," "Taxonomy of City People," "Taxonomy of Highways," "Taxonomy of Things Smaller Than a Fingertip," *ONE ART: a journal of poetry*

"Taxonomy of Wind," *Constellate*

"Taxonomy of Gender," *Human/Kind Journal*

"Taxonomy of Windows," "Taxonomy of Cell Phones," "Taxonomy of Passwords," *NOON: journal of the short poem*

for my brother, Adam

Table of Contents

1.
Taxonomy of Rasps 13
Taxonomy of Gender 14
Taxonomy of Things That Slide 15
Taxonomy of Gloves 16
Taxonomy of Smiles 17
Taxonomy of Silence 18
Taxonomy of Google Autocomplete: *What's the Difference—* 19
Taxonomy of Venom 20
Taxonomy of 70s-Style Recycling 21
Taxonomy of the Pre-Seatbelt Era 22
Taxonomy of Mazes 23
Taxonomy of Taxonomies 24
Taxonomy of Pouches 25
Taxonomy of History 26
Taxonomy of Field Trips 27
Taxonomy of Dancing 28
Taxonomy of Wind 29
Taxonomy of Google Autocomplete: *How Long—* 30
Taxonomy of Cell Phones 31
Taxonomy of Passwords 32
Taxonomy of Late Arrivals 33
Taxonomy of Overheard Conversations 34
Taxonomy of Emptiness 35

2.
Taxonomy of Mica 39
Taxonomy of Moths 40
Taxonomy of Canals 41
Taxonomy of Boats 42
Taxonomy of Churning 43
Taxonomy of Rivers 44
Taxonomy of Mouths 45
Taxonomy of Ears 46

Taxonomy of Headaches.. 47
Taxonomy of Scars.. 48
Taxonomy of Physical Markings.. 49
Taxonomy of Wounds.. 50
Taxonomy of Pre-Existing Conditions... 51
Taxonomy of In-Between.. 52
Taxonomy of Knots.. 53
Taxonomy of Things Smaller Than a Fingertip............................. 54
Taxonomy of Things I Miss.. 55
Taxonomy of Décor.. 56
Taxonomy of Mirages... 57
Taxonomy of *Mid-*... 58
Taxonomy of Menopause.. 59
Taxonomy of Turbulence.. 60

3.
Taxonomy of Places My Work Has Appeared or Is
    Forthcoming.. 63
Taxonomy of Google Autocomplete: *How Far—*............................. 64
Taxonomy of Highways... 65
Taxonomy of City People.. 66
Taxonomy of Quests... 67
Taxonomy of Full Disclosures... 68
Taxonomy of Needles... 69
Taxonomy of Votes... 70
Taxonomy of Fairy Tales... 71
Taxonomy of Recipes.. 72
Taxonomy of Tears... 73
Taxonomy of the Border I... 74
Taxonomy of the Border II.. 75
Taxonomy of Shields... 76
Taxonomy of Nightmares.. 77
Taxonomy of Lockdown.. 78
Taxonomy of Shadows.. 79
Taxonomy of Spills... 80
Taxonomy of Endings That Are Actually Beginnings..................... 81
Taxonomy of Windows... 82
Taxonomy of Google Autocomplete: *How Many—*......................... 83

1.

Taxonomy of Rasps

Bacall telling Bogie it *depends
on who's in the saddle.* Stevie Nicks
insisting nothing else matters.
Kathleen Turner as Jessica Rabbit.
Patti Smith—because the night
belonged to her. A lusty blur of moan
and scold. They didn't ask. They told.

Taxonomy of Gender

A father-to-be aims a rifle
at an explosive target to see
if he's having a boy or a girl.
47,000 acres scorched. 8 million
dollars. And the damage you
cannot see. Every time you say
slaughter, I hear *daughter*.

Taxonomy of Things That Slide

Girl on the playground,
the steel mirror-polished
by the seat of her pants.
Houses after pummeling rains.
Tears. Unwelcome words
about your breasts from men
you pass on the street. Years.

Taxonomy of Gloves

Marshmallow-thick ski gloves.
A pair strung from toddler sleeves.
Lost mate waving from a puddle.
The snapped rubber glove that split open
on the orthodontist's hand. *Ever had
one break on you, dear?* he sneered,
his breath hot in my teen-girl ear.

Taxonomy of Smiles

Ambiguity tugging the seams of Mona Lisa's lips.
Helen of Troy, for surely it wasn't a scowl
that launched a thousand ships. *Smile more*, say men,
always men. But my mouth's default is a grin.
Classic American smile, proclaims my dentist.
What does he mean? Unrestrained? Too much? Larger
than life? When he says *open wider*, I want to bite.

Taxonomy of Silence

Middle of the night stillness. Crisco-thick air
between us after a fight. Reading beside
each other. Ellipses...　　caesuras. The sign
language we taught our baby daughter, the way
she'd press the tips of her fingers together
to insist *more* long after she'd learned to talk,
as if she understood the power in holding back.

Taxonomy of Google Autocomplete:
What's the Difference—

What's the difference between jelly and jam,
between club soda and seltzer, between
a modem and a router? What's the difference
between llamas and alpacas, mildew and mold,
salamanders and newts? What's the difference
between a passport and visa, brown eggs
and white, stars and planets, me and you?

Taxonomy of Venom

Two girls Hula-hooping on the back patio
when a pair of young copperheads comes along.
My father raising the shovel above each one,
then waiting for the mother. The clang of metal
on stone. The blood. The bodies tossed in weeds.
My friend, barefoot and stunned. My father's own
sharp tongue that stings long after he leaves.

Taxonomy of 70s-Style Recycling

My single mother used margarine tubs
for Tupperware, served Kool Aid in jelly jars,
wrapped Pringles cans in tinfoil to transform
a kitchen chair into a birthday throne.
It wasn't about sea turtles or the planet
but the thrill of thrift—something for nothing,
kids without a man, a magic trick.

Taxonomy of the Pre-Seatbelt Era

The summer we moved to Appalachia, gray cat
in one box, my baby brother in another. Me riding
shotgun, protected by my mother's arm. My classmate
Sadie who went through a windshield. I pictured
her floating through a slow-motion spray of glass
stars. How did she stitch *Sadie* from *Sarah?* How did
she find herself behind the constellation of scars?

Taxonomy of Mazes

Diner placemat puzzles, how you learned
to start at the end and work your way back,
avoiding the traps. Maps of arteries glazed
in plaque. Claustrophobic corn mazes
where the frail husk of your body sways
under an autumn sun. Right turn, wrong turn,
turn of phrase. So many ways to lose your way.

Taxonomy of Taxonomies

From the Greek—*taxis:* order, *nomos:* science.
Rules for an unruly world. When my father
slipped into an unclassified black hole, I saved
babysitting money to paint my bedroom walls
yellow. I studied swatches: Sunny Veranda,
Forsythia, Pollen Powder, Gusto Gold,
each strip a family with the same undertones.

Taxonomy of Pouches

Marsupials with built-in Baby Björns.
Velvet bags of prized marbles that look
like eyes. Those overalls we wore
in 8th grade, front pockets so large
they fit textbooks, pens, and tightly
folded notes, freeing our arms for high
fives and everything we hoped to hold.

Taxonomy of History

Those white faces on filmstrips in dark
classrooms, girls passing notes in the back.
How the past is everything that came before:
pyramids and belted maxi pads. The word *circa*
dates to circa 1865, the end of the Civil War.
Or the start, depending on whether you
trust textbooks or what's written in hearts.

Taxonomy of Field Trips

I learned to pack snacks like an American:
family-sized bags of Doritos, 2-liter bottles
of Coke—apples and water a cardinal sin.
Monticello, Williamsburg, D.C. A perennial fave:
the U.S. Mint where sheets of currency coursed
like blood through veins. We were taught to bow
down at the shrine of green money, white men.

Taxonomy of Dancing

The stand and sway. The full-on
stomping and sweating, every limb
flailing as if it's on fire. The train of hands
on hips, stuttering to a stop when a girl
loses a shoe. My college date who said
You're dancing with the drummer, not me.
The burn in my cheeks because it was true.

Taxonomy of Wind

The kind that gives life to kites
and sails. The kind you fight:
headwind on a highway, fuel
needle teetering toward empty.
The kind you want: tailwind,
an invisible nudge from behind
from a mother long, long gone.

Taxonomy of Google Autocomplete:
How Long—

How long is the Great Wall of China?
How long is pink eye contagious, is a dog
in heat? How long is a nap? How long
can you get audited, grow a beard?
How long is an AA meeting? How long
does depression last? How long is
a marathon, a generation, a lightyear?

Taxonomy of Cell Phones

In 1990 BC—Before Cells—I chatted
with a stranger in a laundromat. We've been
friends ever since. Now a communication device
keeps people from talking to each other, our faces
half-aglow in a screen eclipse. We cradle
phones like baby birds who've slipped
from the nest, feed them from our fingertips.

Taxonomy of Passwords

An ex-lover's birthday, the number
of feet in a mile, the number of miles
to her house. *Senha,* Portuguese
for password. The Czech word for hack:
zaseknout. An hour's worth of blows
to a punching bag. The middle name
of the child you never had.

Taxonomy of Late Arrivals

The every-other-weekend father,
his boy at the window practicing
times tables on glass fogged with breath.
In summer: the moon. In winter: the sun.
The girl's date, the one with a blown
muffler and hands that are too quick,
too rough. The next month: her blood.

Taxonomy of Overheard Conversations

Couple at the next table on a blind date,
the high-pitched screech of chair legs on tile
when he stands to leave. Mother and daughter
in a dressing room, the mother saying
You could cover your arm fat with a shawl.
Teenage girl at my gynecologist's office,
her muffled sobs through the thin wall.

Taxonomy of Emptiness

Answer bubbles on a standardized test.
A clean sheet parachuting over
a king-sized bed. Stomachs churning
with hunger or dread. A child's
birthday balloon filled with breath.
How we stitch together the stories
of ourselves with invisible thread.

2.

Taxonomy of Mica

Geological eczema, slivers of silvery
grayish-brown. The shimmer in eye shadow
and metallic paint, glint in South Asian
scarves. *It's complicated* we say now
when relationships are layered, flaking
in our fingers like phyllo pastry shells. How
much can we lose and still be ourselves?

Taxonomy of Moths

Shale confetti flitting against
a white wall. We tried but failed
to make ourselves small, slipping
sideways through doors to leave
them in the night. Moth: so close
to *mouth*. They're drawn to light
like us. Like us, they turn to dust.

Taxonomy of Canals

Panama, Amsterdam, Venice. Root canals.
Birth canals. The C&D Canal where I biked
with my son tucked into a toddler seat
as oceangoing ships from Russia and China
slid by. Such a brief passage. My son waved
to the men on deck. The men waved back.
They were just passing through. We were, too.

Taxonomy of Boats

Speedboats throbbing like hormonal teens.
Sailboats arching like tennis stars.
Skipjacks mumbling like the uncle who sneaks
his own six-pack into the reception hall.
Canoes that poke through shallow waters
like turtles who sun themselves on sunken logs.
They will outlive us. They will outlive us all.

Taxonomy of Churning

The ocean at night: a vast moonlit loom
weaving blue froth. The Delta Queen's
sternwheel muscling through the Mississippi.
Butter on the prairie, Ma teaching Laura
to plunge the dash in stiffening cream.
Voices boiling over on the TV news, so many
words unleashed from what they mean.

Taxonomy of Rivers

The sinewy Mississippi, the Yangtze,
the Nile. Susquehanna, Rappahannock,
Monongahela, Chicopee: words
gurgling over tongues. The sashay
of estuaries, ebbing and flowing
like tango dancers, all moon and mood:
give and take, take and give, love and hate.

Taxonomy of Mouths

Origin of longing, home
for nourishment and song.
How we first connect, lip
and spit and tongue—later,
how we split apart, each word
a volley. Where the river
empties itself into another body.

Taxonomy of Ears

Oyster shell plastered to each side of the head.
Dark canal leading to every story you've heard.
The corner store that detracts teen loiterers
by playing classical music at frequencies
only the young can hear. But not you. You sink
deeper underwater each year. How many
ways to ask *What?* I say *lobe*. You hear *love*.

Taxonomy of Headaches

Road crews chiseling your temples
with pocket-sized jackhammers.
An NBA player palming your skull.
Light like acupuncture needles
in your eyeballs. Tension, hunger,
pollen, hormones. Even your mind
has a mind of its own.

Taxonomy of Scars

Bikini line C-section, the seared
lesson of Caesarean's reversed
a and *e*. Gash between my brows
sowed by years of disbelief. Two
stitches in my knee—5th grade sledding
injury. Big toe, left elbow, right palm.
All the scars you cannot see.

Taxonomy of Physical Markings

Dimples, those adorable genetic defects.
Grandmother puckering a newborn's
toes to check for lucky stars on his feet.
Some people wait their whole lives
to learn from lovers that they're harboring
birthmarks on intimate parts. Some never
find out what it's like to be seen.

Taxonomy of Wounds

The knife slice and cat bite that required tetanus shots. The cocktail of makeup and powder your mother used to cover black eyes. All the men you ever wanted to kill. The skate blade gash that opened your hand like a mouth as if it had secrets to spill.

Taxonomy of Pre-Existing Conditions

The valve that narrows between your brother's
lungs and heart, how he jokes that *stenosis*
sounds like a dinosaur. Your cousin's eczema:
patchwork quilt of flaking scabs. Flat feet.
Allergy to wheat. Fibroids: clusters of birthday
party balloons for the baby who never came to be.
Always waiting to metastasize: grief.

Taxonomy of In-Between

Dawn/dusk. Myth/faith. Love/lust.
Yesterday the two of you were picking
crabs on the back deck. Today, post-stroke,
his brain has *liquified*, the doctors said.
You picture juice—pulverized fruit and kale—
sloshing within the walls of a travel mug.
Minute/year. Grief/relief. Here/not here.

Taxonomy of Knots

My talent for untangling necklaces.
That half-finished scarf, its umbilical
cord of snarled yarn. The newly
discovered twisted squid contorting
in the darkest depths of the Gulf.
My son's varsity soccer teammate
who hanged himself in the barn.

Taxonomy of Things Smaller Than a Fingertip

The Cheerio I tweezed from my son's ear.
The seed of a pumpkin or an idea.
The end of the pen I *clickclickclicked*
waiting to hear—
Battery from my elegant watch that loses
a minute a day. All those minutes stacked
like miniature bricks. All those missed years.

Taxonomy of Things I Miss

Movie theatres with sound
from a single source. The coziness
of telephone booths. Toll collectors
who know the route. Mood rings.
Kids running through sprinklers
on front lawns. The crackle
of a turntable needle between songs.

Taxonomy of Décor

The late-night talk show guest
who drapes scarves across every
corner of her dressing room.
Frank Lloyd Wright re-arranging
hotel furniture as if he were
staying a year. The time it takes
me to say *this belongs here*.

Taxonomy of Mirages

The way desert light bends
to become water: a magic spell.
Trickster mirrors reflecting older
selves. How we're the same bodies
even as we shed and renew our cells.
What I was writing when I thought
I was writing something else.

Taxonomy of *Mid-*

Midsize: the Goldilocks of cars.

Midday: light shows all your scars.

Mid-sentence: when you try—

Mid-semester, mid-winter, mid-thigh.

Mid-century, midnight, midwife.

When every memory is a pang

prying open your heart: midlife.

Taxonomy of Menopause

Estrogen, like Queen Esther from the Bible
if she had spared her people then perished.
You are hollowed out like a cored apple,
a pill bottle with a single tablet rattling inside.
Hole that can't be patched, itch that
scratches back. Everything is burning.
You are on fire and lighting the match.

Taxonomy of Turbulence

Passengers and bags jounce like balls
in a lottery machine. You win if you
walk away cussing but not concussed.
The pilot did not warn us about rough air
or layoffs or divorce or white islands
on an X-ray. He says *Welcome to Boston*
when we thought we'd landed in L.A.

3.

Taxonomy of Places My Work Has Appeared or Is Forthcoming

Tin dish of puréed chicken mixed with fish flakes for my ailing Siamese. Forsythia planted to block the neighbor's trampoline, 'tween heads bobbing above a yellow screen. The hours I've spent making my skin seem naturally *dewy* and *glistening*. Jazz/soul playlist I curated for tonight. I want you to hear it. I want you to hear it without listening.

Taxonomy of Google Autocomplete:
How Far—

How far can you drive on a spare,
walk in a day, cast a fly rod? How far
can you hear a train's whistle, a lion's roar?
How far can you shoot a gun, hear a shot?
How far can you move after divorce? How far
can you see while crying? How far can you
fall? How far can you fall without dying?

Taxonomy of Highways

The ticket I got for driving my 1970
Karmann Ghia too slowly. How my mother
recorded her first trip on the Jersey Turnpike
in her college diary. The motorcyclist
we saw in Sugarloaf, his body smeared
across I-80. How highways pulse with people
who aren't where they want to be.

Taxonomy of City People

How even at 7 a.m. they look polished
in their slim-cut suits and glossy shoes.
How every flick of the wrist seems
pre-ordained: snapping open an umbrella,
scanning a subway pass. Even their hair
knows what to do. Their eyes, too, are
on a mission: not noticing not noticing you.

Taxonomy of Quests

Quixote charging vicious windmills.
Prince Charming and his glass slipper
mission. A widower sweeping the beach
for treasure left behind by tourists
or the tide. Water seeking its own level.
My friend who found his birth mother
three weeks before she died.

Taxonomy of Full Disclosures

Fine print in bank loans. Side effects
in drug ads. Your asset to debt ratio,
the last forbidden food you had.
The number of times you masturbated
this week. A secret glove compartment
gun. Four true words I could say
to make you cry, five to make you run.

Taxonomy of Needles

The glint of silver in the haystack.
The eye through which you try to fit
a camel. Thread and mended jeans.
Veins and vaccines. One needle heals—
another numbs. The track marks
on your sister's arms: calligraphy
of bird claws, trail of stale breadcrumbs.

Taxonomy of Votes

In some countries, they dip index fingers in ink
to show who voted. *Electoral stain.* Here, we pull levers
like slot machines. *God gave us sports and weather
so we don't have to talk politics,* a friend complained.
But I don't care about baseball or rain. Remember
the *hanging chads*, assonant as a garage band name?
Their songs are IEDs that echo in your brain.

Taxonomy of Fairy Tales

Humpty Dumpty chants
Build that wall. The piper
lures all the rats to town.
The huntsman targets
everyone who isn't white
as snow. The wolf huffs & puffs
& blows the world down.

Taxonomy of Recipes

Soufflés are tragic. Hollandaise is a breeze.
For a challenge, turn a sweet savory or a savory
sweet. Everything tastes better with chicken broth.
Directions are optional except when they're not.
A macaroon is not a macaron, and neither one
is president of France. Our own sad concoction
of leaders forgot we're a melting pot.

Taxonomy of Tears

Loss, of course, but also allergies,
eye drops, onions. And laughter,
especially in the classroom of a stern
teacher. Swallow it. Hold it in. Do. Not.
Look. At. Your. Friend. And clouds
of gas: streams on cheeks of children
with bare feet, white diapers, brown skin.

Taxonomy of the Border I

They took the children from their mothers. They ignored their cries. The children's cries. The mothers' cries. They took the children from their mothers. Babies in diapers, cocooned in woven senkas, girls with pink butterfly barrettes, boys in red Elmo shirts, children with sleep in their eyes.

Taxonomy of the Border II

They took the shoes from the children,
gnawed off gummy soles with knives
like whittlers on the porch of a shotgun
house. They slipped laces from the throats
of sneakers and boots, then handed back husks
of canvas and rubber as if to say *Only we have
the power, the power to make a noose.*

Taxonomy of Shields

Plastic eyepatch after cataract surgery.
Burglar alarms, pepper spray, air bags.
Antibacterial wipes, vitamins, a seat
in first class. School buses full of bullet-
proof backpacks. Foreheads crossed with ash.
How we try to inoculate ourselves against
being shattered in a world made of glass.

Taxonomy of Nightmares

A man chases you in a revolving door.
You are falling, falling and open your eyes
right before you hit the floor. A dark alley,
a gun. You forget to take an exam—or later,
to give one. Teeth fall out like unstrung beads.
Your car has no brakes. The nightmare
in which you realize it's scarier to be awake.

Taxonomy of Lockdown

Sanitize touchpoints with Clorox wipes,
stock the pantry with beans & rice. Patch cracked
plaster you see when still. Try not to kill your mate
who chews like a horse galloping on gravel. If masks
fog your glasses, wipe the hazy half-moons hiding
your eyes. Each day is a recipe of equal parts
boredom and fear. Knead a ball of anger. Let it rise.

Taxonomy of Shadows

Lean companion strolling beside you
on the beach. Alter ego. Body to the soul.
The man who sold his shadow to the devil.
Shadowless demons. Your twin crow.
The shadow Peter Pan lost and Wendy
reattached. The darkness that pools
around statues celebrating our dark past.

Taxonomy of Spills

Milk, but don't cry over it. Black opal
ooze of oil, birds trapped in slick
straightjackets. What's the phrase
for saying too much? *Spilled his heart?*
No—as if truth is violence—*spilled his guts.*
Guns kill 100 souls a day. We are all
slipping on sidewalks thick with blood.

Taxonomy of Endings That Are Actually Beginnings

The last scene of *The Godfather*,
when the closed door shows Michael's
transformation into the boss. Cilantro
that *bolts* mid-summer, leaving behind
coriander seeds. False sunrise teasing
the real thing. The man who knew your mom
was pregnant and left. A knee on the neck.

Taxonomy of Windows

Floor-to-ceiling glass overlooking
a beach you claim to own. Below-deck
portholes on your 100-foot yacht.
Boarded-up windows of a house
on a block in a city left to rot.
An interrogation room's one-way view.
Where were you? Where were you?

Taxonomy of Google Autocomplete:
How Many—

How many stripes on a zebra?
How many cups in a quart, feet in
a mile, minutes in a day? How many
years to paint the Sistine Chapel?
How many lives lost in Iraq, children
poisoned in Flint? How many,
how many look the other way?

Erin Murphy is the author of seven previous books of poetry, most recently *Assisted Living*, and co-editor of three anthologies, including *Bodies of Truth: Personal Narratives on Illness, Disability, and Medicine*, winner of the 2019 Foreword INDIES Book of the Year Award. Her poems and essays have been published in *Women's Studies Quarterly, The Best of Brevity, Rattle, Waxwing, Southern Humanities Review, Laurel Review, Contrary, The Georgia Review,* and *Guesthouse* and featured on *The Writer's Almanac*. Her awards include The Normal School Poetry Prize, the Dorothy Sargent Rosenberg Poetry Prize, and a Best of the Net award. She serves as Poetry Editor of *The Summerset Review* and is Professor of English and Creative Writing at Penn State Altoona where she has received the university-wide Alumni Award for Excellence in Teaching. Website: www.erin-murphy.com

Made in the USA
Middletown, DE
11 June 2022

66849012R00052